Aquaponics At Home

Growing Fish & Vegetables

By Amber Richards

Copyright © Amber Richards 2014 All Rights Reserved. No part of this book may be reproduced without our express consent.

Table of Contents

What is Aquaponics?	1
Basic Components needed for an Aquaponics System	7
Choosing the Plants for an Aquaponics System	12
Choosing the Fish for an Aquaponics System	17
Benefits of Aquaponics Systems	27
Setting up an Aquaponic System	33
Short on Space – Build a Mini Aquaponics System	43
Vertical Aquaponics Systems	53
Maintaining the Aquaponics System	59
Interesting Facts about Aquaponics	61
Conclusion	65

What is Aquaponics?

A combination of hydroponics, which is growing plants with water instead of soil and aquaculture or raising fish is known as aquaponics. When correctly set up, aquaponics can be used to create a symbiotic system where plants, fish and bacteria live together and mutually benefit from the presence of each other.

Commonly, fresh water fish are used for aquaponics. The bacteria present is good bacteria that aids in breaking down waste from the fish. The plants grow in a soil-less environment and are fertilized by the waste excrement from the fish. Plants also tend to grow very rapidly in this type of situation. In return, the plants oxygenate and clean the water, and it is then re-circulated back to the fish.

Typically, only the water that is evaporated from the plants, needs to be replaced, roughly 2% every week or so. Once a system is set up, the maintenance is fairly low.

Both the fish and the vegetables or other types of plants grown are used as a healthy food source.

Some forms of aquaponics can be dated back to as early as some of the Aztec civilizations.

However, aquaponics seems to be making a modern come-back in more recent years.

Many nations are actively educating their people on the practice of aquaponics to both increase healthy, clean food supplies, and decrease the need to import food. In Barbados in particular, they are also encouraged to sell their grown vegetables to tourists to help families increase their income levels additionally.

With more and more people desiring a more self-sustainable lifestyle and/or living off the grid, aquaponics is a popular option. It is a good use of space, and can be adjusted to individual goals and situations. It can be for the person who intends to go large scale on a commercial basis, to the person who lives in a condo and simply wants this as both an enjoyable hobby with additional to freshly grown, organic vegetables or herbs, and fish.

There are several ways to build a system using items that can be purchased from your local hardware store. Some of the most popular will be explained in the following chapters. I will also share a few links for you to compare notes for different system setups, as these seem to vary quite abit from person to person. My hope is that by gleaning information from a variety of sources, you'll be able to fine tune what will work best for your specific situation.

Here's an image of some lettuce roots that used a system using styrofoam as a growing medium. As you can see, the root systems are long, well developed and supporting healthy plants.

Basic Components needed for an Aquaponics System

The tank – This can be an actual fish tank made of glass or plexiglass. You may also use a container such as a plastic tote, bucket or tub. Some people prefer a clear container because it makes it easier to see the fish. The size of the container will depend on the size of the aquaponics system being built. Generally they are from 3 to 20 gallons or larger if you prefer. Larger tanks allow larger growing areas.

Pea gravel, clay pebbles, perlite, or peat moss is the material used, often called the growing medium. It is what contains the roots of the plants and allows them to hold moisture needed for growing. There is also a grow medium many people opt to use called Hydroton (example can be seen at http://www.amazon.com/gp/product/B000FCPDFA) that is used in hydroponic and aquaponic systems. It is basically clay pebbles, but a popular choice.

Gravel – This is used in the bottom of the fish tank or container that will hold the fish. It is where the bacteria lives that converts the ammonia from the fish to nitrite and nitrate. It is then used by the plants. The gravel should be thoroughly rinsed before using it because it has dust that will cause your fish tank water to become cloudy.

Grow bed – This is the container that will be used to hold the pea gravel, clay pebbles, perlite, or peat moss for holding the roots of the plants. It should be from 3 to 8 inches deep and fit on top of the aquarium. This container can be plastic or it can be made of plexiglass as long as it is leak-proof.

Water pump and tubing – This pump will carry the water from the fish tank to the grow container. The water pumped into the container will be gravity-fed back into the fish tank. This is why enough tubing will be needed to go from the pump to the top of the grow container and loop around the inside.

Air pump, tubing and air stone – The air pump will connect to the air stone using the tubing and it will pull air into the fish tank benefiting the plants and the fish. The air stone makes micro-bubbles that rise in the fish tank and creates more oxygen in the water.

The fish and the plants – The fish provide nutrients needed by plants and in turn, the plants consume these nutrients, which purifies the water. You will also need proper fish food for the specific fish you decide to raise. Some people plant sprouted seeds, some plant seedlings of young plants, and some plant just the seeds of what they want to grow.

Optional - Some individuals choose to use standard individual plastic grow pots for their plants, within their grow beds.

Most of these supplies can be purchased at various garden supply stores, or online retailers such as amazon.com.

Choosing the Plants for an Aquaponics System

What plants are best for suited for aquaponics? There are a variety of plants that can be used such as lettuce, cabbage, fruits, vines and flowers. The most often grown are lettuce, cabbage, peas and even green beans.

Others include:

Tomatoes

Squash

Bell Peppers

Cucumbers

Strawberries

Kale

Okra

Melons

Celery

Snow peas

Herbs

Vines also do well in this type of system. Flowers such as lilies and roses are good choices.

Some of the herbs that are grown in aquaponic systems include sage, coriander, watercress, parsley, lemon grass, basil, oregano, capsicum and basically any type of plant that likes to have wet roots.

You may be surprised at how good vegetables taste because they are grown organically and allowed to ripen naturally. Supplements for the plants can include natural ones such as seaweed extract. It is important that you be careful when adding supplements because certain types can cause problems with fish and bacteria and ruin the entire system. Allow the fish you choose time to fertilize the water with their waste and plants will thrive.

There are more than 300 plants that are suitable for aquaponics. This is to say, that more than this amount have been tested for use in the systems and do quite well. The ones that do not work as well typically, are root vegetables such as potatoes, onions or carrots, but even those can be grown in the correct situation. Herbs and leafy vegetables are most commonly chosen because they do very well. It will also depend on whether your aquaponics system is inside or outdoors. Some people choose to put them in a garage or on a covered patio, in the backyard or in a greenhouse.

Plants grown in an aquaponic environment often have growth rates that are far better than typical growing conditions. This is due to the plants being in an aquaponic system getting as much water and organic fertilizer (fresh waste) as is needed; whereas plants grown in the ground may use all available water especially when the weather is hot. The continuous flow of water as well as drainage in an aquaponic system contributes to better growth.

Romaine Lettuce

Choosing the Fish for an Aquaponics System

Fish are very important to an aquaponic system. One, they provide the nutrients needed by the plants being grown. Two, if you are growing the fish to eat, they provide another food source in addition to the vegetables. This can be a fairly simple endeavor and some people say growing fish in an aquaponics system is easier than growing them in an aquarium. Some of the following fish are grown just for their ornamental aspects while others are grown as a source of food.

What types of fish are best for growing?

Barramundi are one type that are generally grown in warm months. Choose mature fish and this will allow larger fish to be harvested at the end of the growing season. These fish, when grown in an aquaponics system, have a very good taste.

Goldfish are another type that are grown by many people. They can be found at most pet shops and are considered pretty easy to raise. They are a hardy fish that will reproduce as long as they have plants in which to breed.

Catfish come in a variety of species and they are easy to grow in an aquaponics system. The type that is most often grown is the channel catfish.

They grow quickly and are very tasty. They will need to be skinned when preparing them for eating because they do not have scales.

The Jade Perch is native to Australia and is often grown for eating because of their high omega three oil content. Omega three fatty oils provide a number of health benefits. Although some people do not care for oily fish, this type grows rapidly and are easily obtainable. They are more suited to a warm water aquaponics system, so one that is in a very temperate climate or using a heater is optimal for growing Jade Perch.

Murray Cod are another fish that is native to Australia and will grow quite large. They also grow quickly and are excellent for eating. When choosing this type to grow in an aquaponics system, they must be kept well fed because they will eat each other if not.

Tilapia are one of the most popular for aquaponics systems. This is because they grow quickly, are great breeders and are delicious. In addition, they can survive in less than desirable water conditions as well as being known for their varied appetite. They can eat practically anything. They do prefer warm water so a heater or living in a warm climate is important for growing Tilapia.

Carp are known for being tough and they can adapt to virtually any condition. They are considered nuisance fish to some, but there are many different species that are very well suited to growing in aquaponics systems. There are also some places that do not allow keeping them and the fines for doing so can be quite high, so be sure to research that point further if you want to use carp.

Another fish that is considered popular is trout. They like water temperatures to be somewhat cool, generally between 50 and 60 degrees. This fish grow quickly and are very tasty; a couple of reasons for their popularity.

Although most people do not realize it , Koi are a species of carp. They are ornamental fish and can be used in an aquaponics system for the enjoyment of watching and learning from them. They are very popular for ponds and the ideal water temperature range is from 65 to 75 degrees.

There are other aquatic animals that can aid in keeping an aquaponic system running smoothly. They include fresh water crayfish, prawns and mussels. Crustaceans can also be used depending on water temperature. Redclaw is one that prefers warmer water temperatures, while Marron or Yabbies can be introduced into systems with cooler water. They help to filter the water and keep the system running smoothly. Yabbies will eat each other if there are too many in one tank.

The number of fish that are kept in a tank will have an effect on the system. Generally the higher the number, the more likely it is that something will go wrong. When keeping a large number of fish, it is very important to keep a check on water conditions constantly to prevent problems. Keeping the number of fish to a lower level also provides more growing room for the plants.

Smallmouth Bass, Crappie, Chinese Catfish, and Bluegill are a few more types recommended for aquaponics. There are several others that can be chosen depending on the climate and the rules for growing particular types of fish within your state or country.

Aquaponics At Home

Tilapia Fish

Benefits of Aquaponics Systems

There are several benefits to aquaponic gardening. In addition to raising fish and vegetables for consumption, this form of gardening provides faster growing rates. They actually grow about three times faster than plants grown in soil. You can also plant more in smaller spaces. The amount of water that is used is also less because it is recirculated. You need only replace what evaporates and the amount used by the plants. An abundant supply of fruits, vegetables and fish are all available from your home.

Aquaponic gardening does not require a lot of work when compared to traditional gardening. There is no need to weed, fertilize or water the plants. Additionally, the system is set up at a higher level so there is no strain on your back from bending over to tend to the plants. You do not have to use a sprinkler system to water the plants during dry spells. The energy expended for an aquaponic system is a small amount to run the pump for the water.

Fertilizing is not necessary as the waste excrements of the fish fertilize the plants. The system can be set up anywhere from your basement to the back yard or greenhouse. This is a good project for schools and neighborhood centers as well. As a learning experience, this can be a valuable lesson for students on growing their own food without the need for pesticides or other harmful chemicals. Because of the natural growing conditions, the fish and vegetables are considered healthier and safer than using alternative methods. Fish is a very good source of protein and the vegetables have loads of essential nutrients.

In addition, fish provide omega-3 fatty acids, which are very beneficial for overall health. The benefits of omega-3 fatty acids include decreasing the risk of heart disease, increasing good cholesterol by lowering triglycerides and lowering blood pressure. Additionally, they are thought to aid in preventing the accumulation of a protein that is related to Alzheimers.

The setup of an aquaponics system can be as small or as large as needed. If space is a concern a small system can be easily fit into a corner and for large operations, using the same principles, the system can be adapted to fit a commercial application. Even if affordability is a concern, there is a system that can be constructed from used materials. From recycled aquariums to food shipping containers, there are all types of materials that can be used to build an aquaponic system. The systems are cost effective because the major expense will be feeding the fish. Also, the basic instructions for setting everything up can be followed quite easily even if you have very little experience with do-it-yourself projects.

Aquaponics does not use pesticides; therefore, the vegetables and fruits that are grown using this method are healthier, especially for children. The environment is another aspect that benefits from aquaponics since pesticides are not present to leach into water supplies or pollute the air.

Due to the fact that there are no weeds growing near the plants, there is no competition for nutrients. The fruits and vegetables get all of them. The plants do not get the diseases that can plague those in traditional settings likely due to increased nutrition.

Setting up an Aquaponic System

What is the basic way of setting up a tank or container for the fish and plants? There are several types that can be used. We will explore three of them so you can choose the one that best suits the space you have available. They are not expensive to build and the benefits that will be reaped are many.

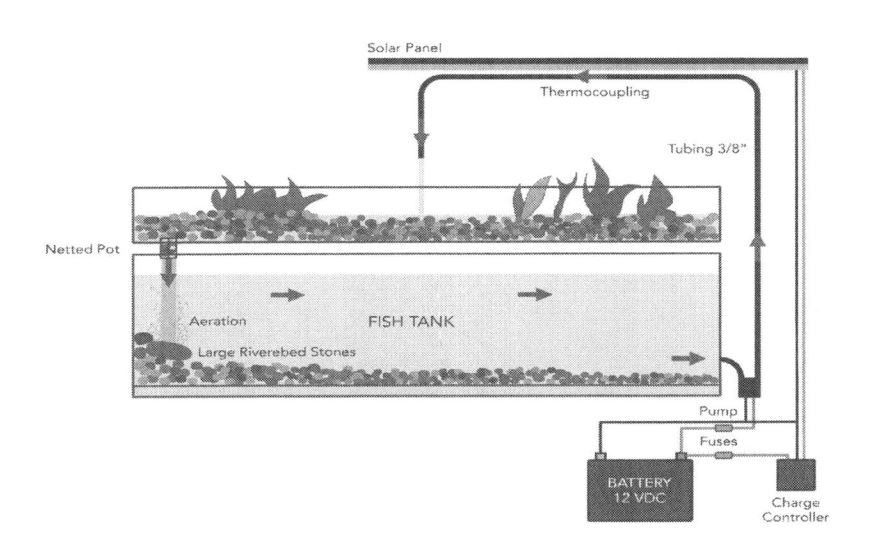

Media filled beds or the type that uses a growing medium are the most popular type of aquaponic systems. Both the systems explained above are examples of this type of aquaponic system. There are also Deep Water Culture (DWC) and Nutrient Film Technique (NFT) systems. The DWC method floats the plants being used on top of the water with their roots hanging in the water. This method is often used in commercial aquaponics systems. The plants can be placed in foam containers that sit on top of the fish tank.

The NFT system is mainly used for leafy green vegetables because other plants' root systems are too large for this system. The plants are placed in plastic cups that give their roots access to water that flows through small gutters in a thin film. This method is also not suitable for plants that get large because they often become too heavy for the cups.

The following method is a simple aquaponic system that can be set up using items that are readily available and it is great for indoors.

Find a frame that will hold wire baskets and plastic containers. If you cannot find one readily available you can build one using the dimensions of the containers and baskets as a guide. A 13-gallon container is good for a fish tank and a 6 to 7 gallon container can be used for the grow bed. The wire baskets are reinforcement for the plastic containers that you will be using. If you plan to put the container for the fish on the floor, you should not need a wire basket as the floor will provide the support needed.

You can use a fish tank made from glass or plexiglass. Ten or 20-gallon tanks can be used, depending on the size of the grow bed you desire. The rule of thumb for this is usually 1 to 2 feet of growing area for each 10 gallons of water in a fish tank.

A small submersible pump (an example is http://www.amazon.com/gp/product/B006M6MSL0) is perfect to use in a corner of the fish tank for pumping the water from the fish tank to the grow bed. The water will flow into the grow bed and exit through a corner opposite the one used for the submersible pump. This can be easily constructed using a male and female adapter with threads. A hole should be drilled in the corner about 2 ½ inches from both sides of the container. The male adapter should fit snugly in this hole. Put a rubber o-ring on the threads of the of the male adapter and screw the female adapter onto the male adapter. This allows the fit to be waterproof. Next place a reducer on the top of the male adapter.

In effect you are creating a standpipe, which is responsible for allowing the water to exit the grow bed. It should stand about an inch above the top of the grow bed plants. This is a type of standpipe that is easy to make and it has no moving parts so it holds up very well.

Now you will construct a bell siphon for carrying water to the grow bed. It will do so slowly and it is also responsible for draining the grow bed rapidly. This is constructed of a piece of pipe with a cap at the top that provides an air-tight fit. The pipe should have one-inch holes drilled in the sides beginning about an inch from the bottom. This will allow the water to drain to this level and stop.

The bell siphon (an example is at http://www.amazon.com/gp/product/B00BPF1K

DU) will be placed in the middle of the grow bed. A guard is also needed and can be constructed of a piece of 100mm pipe with holes drilled to allow the water to enter, but it keeps other things such as the growing medium out of the bell siphon. The growing medium is the material used to hold the roots of the plants as well as moisture. Some items that may be used include pea gravel, perlite, peat moss or coconut coir. This can be placed on the far right side of the grow bed. A short video example showing more about a bell siphon can be seen at http://www.youtube.com/watch?v=gFokOynqOqQ.

Next you will need a ball-valve by-pass. This is how you will control the amount of water flowing into the grow bed and it helps to redirect some of the water back to the fish tank. This aids in aerating the tank as well as moving the water, which is important to the health of the fish. The pump will be attached to the end of a 13mm pipe and a T-valve can be attached about a third of the way up the pipe. A ball-valve by-pass is added to the pipe just past the t-valve. This will allow you to control the flow of the water.

Elbows are added to the pipe so that it comes up from the fish tank at the bottom and makes the turns to the grow bed at the top. The pipe is attached to the submersible pump in the tank.

Once this is all set up and the water is added to the fish tank, the pump can be started and the system can be tested to ensure that everything is working properly and there are no leaks. If everything is okay, a couple of fish can be added to begin with and they will produce the ammonia needed to get the system started.

Of course you have the option to also purchase a ready made kit, or plumbing kit to get started.

There are so many options for building your own aquaponics system, that further research should be done after defining your goals and the space you have to dedicate to the project. If you studied 100 aquaponic systems, most likely all

100 would be different. When its all said and done, any system that works correctly, will do.

Here are a couple other options of how different individuals have set up their systems to give a visual aid.

Kitchen Aquaponics http://youtu.be/-8H30hFkVwk

Aquaponics Planting - Kale http://youtu.be/x0XhYJwBdjE

Aquaponics Garden Cheap http://youtu.be/ltrqsn1nR9E

Aquaponic Grow Bed Instruction http://youtu.be/Q7EVYGFTxwg

Short on Space – Build a Mini Aquaponics System

As mentioned previously, an aquaponics system can be as small as needed. If you are short of space, here is a mini system that while it will not provide fish for consumption, it can provide many vegetables, fruits and herbs for your kitchen. This is a system that can be used as a teaching tool as well with the principles being put to use for a larger system at a later date.

What you will Need:

1. A small tank or plastic or glass container – from 3 to 20 gallon

2. Water pump (example http://www.amazon.com/gp/product/B000CKFAZS) – a small capacity, 4-watt will do nicely

3. Aquarium air pump, example http://www.amazon.com/gp/product/B004PB8SMM/

4. Plastic tubing for the water pump – approximately 3 feet

5. Plastic tubing for the air pump – approximately 3 feet

6. Grow container – 4 to 8 inches deep

7. Gravel – for each 5 gallons of water the tank holds, use 2 ½ pounds of gravel

8. Air stone (example http://www.amazon.com/gp/product/B003UPOXXC) – 1 to 3 inch

9. Pea gravel, clay pebbles, perlite, or peat moss – enough to fill the grow container

10. pH test kit (example http://www.amazon.com/gp/product/B000255NAK)

11. Fish

12. Plants or seeds

13. Growing Medium - enough pea gravel, perlite, coconut coir, expanded clay pebbles or peat moss to fill the grow bed ($2 - $5)

14. Electrical tape

15. Drill – 1/4", 1/8" and 1/2" bits

16. Scissors

If you want there are a few optional items that can also be used for your aquaponic system. A heater for the aquarium or container used for the fish is necessary if the fish you choose are tropical. They generally need the water temperature to be about 78 degrees. The heater can be a submersible type or one that mounts on the side of the tank. If you are going to put tropical fish in your tank or if you just want to be able to watch the fish, a fluorescent light is another necessity.

If you will be setting up your system in an area that is not well lit, you may want to purchase a grow light for your plants. However, this does encourage algae growth in the fish tank, so an algae-eating fish can be a good investment to help keep the tank clean. Snails also do a good job.

Begin by washing the gravel for the tank and place it in the bottom. Next using your drill and the 1/8" drill bit, drill holes about 2 inches apart in the bottom of the grow container. They will allow the water to drain into the fish tank. In a back corner of the grow container drill a hole using the 1/2" bit for the tubing for the water pump.

Put the water pump in the fish tank and put the grow container on top of the tank. Push the tubing for the water pump through the hole in the grow container, leaving enough to stick up about three-fourths of the height of the container and loop around the inside. Fold it over and seal with electrical tape. Add the pea gravel, clay pebbles, perlite, or peat moss you will be using almost all the way up in grow container. Use a small sharp object to punch holes about every 2 inches in the tubing looped around the inside of the container. Finish filling the container with the pea gravel, clay pebbles, perlite, or peat moss.

Next put water in the fish tank and plug in the pump to make sure the water being pumped into the grow container is soaking the material used in the grow bed and going back into the tank. This may need to be adjusted. The air pump can be connected to the air stone using the tubing. Put the air stone in the tank and plug in the pump. If it is working correctly, bubbles should rise in the water. This will provide air to the tank.

Check the pH of the water. It should be 7.0. This may need to be adjusted as well. It can be raised or lowered using products found in your local aquarium supply store. At this point, the water contains chlorine if it has been filled using tap water and needs to sit for at least 24 hours before adding fish. You can also purchase chlorine remover from your aquarium supply store if you do not want to wait 24 hours.

Fish can be put into the fish tank once the chlorine has dissipated. Start with only a couple and increase the amount in about a month. You should only have 1 fish for every gallon held by the tank. If it is a five-gallon tank, five fish are sufficient. The plants should really not be added until about a month after the system has been up and running. However, if you simply cannot wait, add a couple to start and you can put more in after about 4 to 6 weeks. The entire cost of putting together this system is about $125.

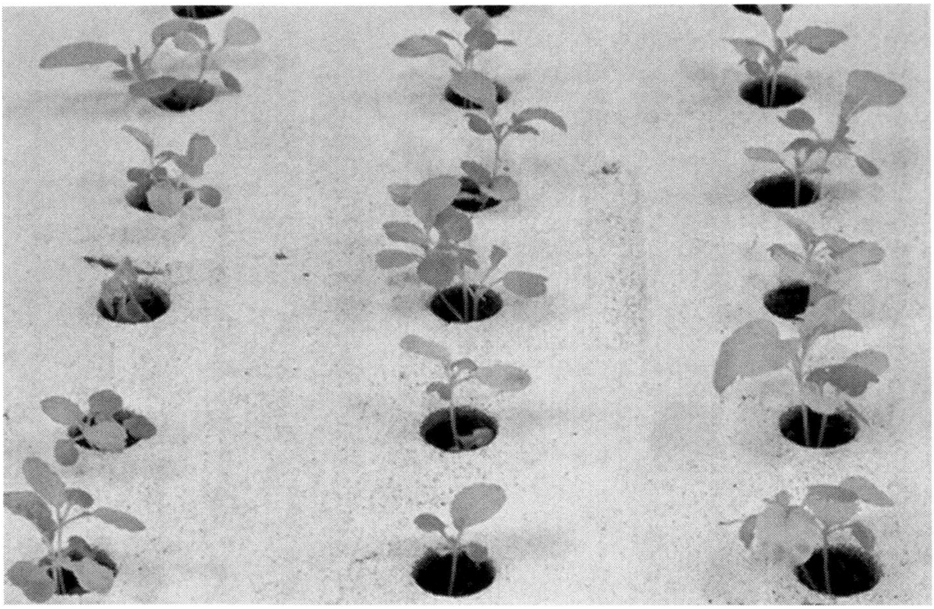

Vertical Aquaponics Systems

A vertical aquaponics system uses less water and produces more food. As a matter of fact, the amount produced is about twice that of hydroponic gardening. Growing vertically also saves space. This system has also aptly been named "barrelponics" due to the use of barrels.

Here is a video demonstration of a setup of a vertical aquaponics system http://youtu.be/AaKDQiWYJow.

What is needed to build a vertical system?

Aquarium pump

Air pump

Tubing for the aquarium pump and the air pump – about 20 feet

4-inch PVC – approximately 20 feet

4-inch T connects – four of these

4-inch elbows – four of these

2 50-gallon drums

Plastic cups

Cloth

Fasteners – cable ties are fine

The PVC pipe should be cut into 6 one-foot sections, except for two pieces that should be 14 inches long. Drill two holes in each of the one-foot sections. They should be three inches in diameter. Drill a hole in the side of one of the 14-inch pieces. The hole should be about 1 inch in diameter. Put these pieces together using electrical tape. This can consist of one of the 1-foot sections, a T-connect, another 1-foot section, another T-connect and another 1-foot section. Next connect an elbow and then a 14-inch section and another elbow and follow the same pattern around the other side and the other end.

Cut pieces of pipe to approximately three-foot sections and drill 1-inch holes in these sections, making sure they are spaced evenly. Place the three-foot sections of pipe in the T-connects of the original frame. Punch some holes in the bottom of the plastic cups and set them into the holes you drilled in the one-foot sections of pipe. A piece of pipe can be cup and placed in the hole made earlier in the 14-inch piece of pipe. This will serve as a drain.

Set the entire frame on the two 50-gallon barrels with the drain over one of the barrels. Start seedlings in peat pods that can be placed in the cups. The tubing should be attached to the pump in one of the barrels and to each of the four 3-foot sections of pipe that were placed in the Tconnections. This barrel is where your fish will live. Another pump can be placed into the drain barrel and the water can be pumped back to the fish tank.

For more growing space, cloth can be torn into strips and tied to the top of each 3-foot section of pipe and drop them inside the pipe. Put peat pods in the holes drilled in the sections of 3-foot pipe. They will use the cloth for stabilizing the roots as the plants grow. As the water is pumped up through the standing pipes and the bottom ones in which the cups were placed, the plants will receive the nutrient rich water from the fish tank. It will drain into the other barrel and be recirculated.

Maintaining the Aquaponics System

Most aquaponics systems are simple to maintain. This is why they have become so popular. Fish should be fed daily and small amounts are better than large amounts. A pinch is all that is needed unless your tank is huge. If you have tropical fish, the flake food is sufficient. Blood worms or brine shrimp can be given occasionally.

The water will need to be replaced as it evaporates and is used by the plants. This should only need to be done about 1 to 2 times per week. Each month, it is a good idea to take out about 15% of the water from the fish tank and replace it with fresh water. Make sure you use treated water or have some on hand that has set for at least 24 hours so it does not contain chlorine.

Generally the time it takes to maintain your system will be less than five minutes a day and ten to fifteen minutes weekly. About twice a month, the aeration stone and the bottom of the pump should be rinsed. Ensuring that everything is functioning as it should takes only a couple of minutes. Compared to traditional gardening, you will spend far less time with aquaponics systems. The fun part will be harvesting your fish and food produce for eating.

Smallmouth Bass Fish

Interesting Facts about Aquaponics

Although modern aquaponics is still fairly new, it was used in ancient times. Some of the first examples are thought to be islands where plants raised with water and other materials from the Chinampa canals. The islands, known as Chinampas were mainly stationary, but some were movable. Also, rice was raised in Thailand and China in paddies, which also contained fish. Other Far Eastern countries also raised fish – Swamp eels, regular and Crucian Carp, and Oriental Loach – in rice paddies.

Because fish do not all require the same things when it comes to the water in which they live, research is ongoing into what would be required to grow different types of fish. Some require different water temperatures and the pH levels are also different. Two that can be raised together are prawns and Tilapia.

The use of aquaponics allows people to grow food and raise fish, which is a very beneficial and incredible way of being able to sustain oneself. They can do so using less than 330 feet of space. A large aquaponic system that is capable of growing 5000 plants weekly can allow earnings of more than $1300 per week with only 2 hours of work per day. The most profitable plants grown using aquaponics systems are basil, Chinese cabbage, tomatoes, lettuce, bell peppers, okra, cantaloupe and roses.

Many vegetables grown using aquaponics systems have a growing cycle that is much shorter than growing them the traditional way.

For example, cucumbers grown using this method take less than one month to mature. Watercress, ginger, mint, tomatoes, papayas and nasturtiums are others that have shown to grow more rapidly when using aquaponics.

The use of indoor systems and vertical systems are becoming more popular as they would allow growing food all year. Because aquaponics only requires that water be added due to evaporation, the use by plants and in some instances overflow from rain, the amount of water used is about 2% of the amount required by conventional farming for the same vegetable production.

Conclusion

Before deciding if an aquaponics system is right for your needs, there are a few things that should be taken into consideration. Ask yourself a few of the following questions to help in narrowing down what you want from an aquaponics system.

Do you want to raise fish for eating? Which ones are your favorites? Are you more interested in the fruits, vegetables or flowers? If so, what vegetables should be grown? Most people prefer certain types of vegetables and fruits over others. For example, are tomatoes a favorite or do you eat a lot of salads? How much do you want to grow? Is the aquaponic system going to be a hobby or are you planning to grow food to supplement what is purchased?

Do you have the space for the type that you are interested in building? If you live in an apartment, a small system for growing herbs may be a better choice. Since aquaponics yield more than traditional gardening, will you be able to use everything that is grown? It is also important to remember that the systems can take a while to get everything to the ideal conditions needed to grow plants. If the system will be outdoors, the time of year that it is started should be considered.

Growing the food that you and your family will eat will provide you with a sense of satisfaction. Even more importantly, knowing that it was grown naturally and without the chemicals often used in traditional gardening will provide peace of mind.

By Amber Richards

If you enjoyed this book or received value from it in any way, would you be kind enough to leave a review for this book on Amazon? I would be so grateful. Thank you!

Made in the USA
Middletown, DE
13 November 2019